THE 5:22 MAN

By: Gregory L. Bloomfield

Printed in the United States of America

ISBN: 978-0-578-33082-2

Graphic Design, Formatting, and Interior Layout

D. F. G. Publishing House LLC.

DFGPUBLISHING2021@GMAIL.COM

www.dfgpublishingtoday.com

Contents

Acknowledgements

First, I must acknowledge my Lord and Savior, Jesus Christ, for all of the blessings that He has given me throughout my life. During the ups and the downs, He has always been faithful.

Next, like most Black men, I must acknowledge my mother, Patsy McGlashan aka Sister Pamella. Thank you so much for being the epitome of strength and faith in Christ and for being a wonderful living epistle for me.

Thank you to my two heartbeats ... my son, Thaddeus Bloomfield and my daughter, Isabelle Bloomfield. I am incredibly proud to be your father and I pray that you are as equally proud of me with this book.

To my brothers, Kyle Bloomfield, Michael James and Anton James. Each of you are amazing men and I am proud to be your brother.

To my brothers from different mothers ... Craige Campbell and Richard Lambie. With over 30 years of friendship, thank you for being such an inspiration to my life and true friends and examples of incredible men.

To every pastor who has mentored me and shepherd me from a little kid to right now. Thank you.

Big shout outs to the Attleboro SDA Men's Ministry group, and the Merrimack Valley SDA Men's Ministry Group Thank you for your friendship, fellowship and accountability. We are changing the lives of men ... one person at a time.

To every woman of God that has poured into me and corrected me in love when I was messing up. Thank you! Every good man needs a team of wise women because they can see things that we cannot.

And most importantly, thank you to my late father ... Withbourne "Dan" Leonard Bloomfield. I know that if he were still here, he would be so proud of me. He is the true 5:22 Man.

If I did not mention you specifically, you know that you are special to me. Thank you!!!

Enjoy this publication ... the 5:22 Man. I pray that this blesses you and changes your life while you read it.

Introduction

———— ✥ ————

"Thank you, Mr. Bloomfield. I think you have completed all the necessary paperwork. Here are the keys to your new townhouse," said Whitney at the management office. I told Whitney thank you as well and took the keys. The next day, I and a few of my friends from my church loaded the U-Haul truck with all my stuff from the church family I was staying with for a few weeks after I was separated from my wife of four years. I must admit that it was fun to be with my church family, and the people I stayed with were an older couple from the South, both of whom had experienced divorce themselves. They imparted wisdom and empowered me for the next part of my life journey. In fact, I moved into the same neighborhood they lived in when they first moved up from the South to Massachusetts, where I currently live.

After my friends moved my stuff into the house and said goodbye, I was in my townhouse . . . Alone. I went upstairs to the master bedroom and took a hard look at myself, and honestly, I began to cry. "Another failed marriage? Are you serious? Gregory, you screwed up again!" You see, for those of you who have never been married before, it goes like this: Nobody who gets married plans to get separated and divorced. Unfortunately, it happened to me . . . twice. The first time was bad enough because I believed that I had married the love of my life, and even though we were young, we were Christians and could overcome anything. I grew up in the church, so how could I make mistakes as a husband, right? We divorced after eleven years of marriage, leaving two little kids to figure out why Dad moved out and wonder if Mommy and Daddy would ever get back together. Then I got married again five years later, saying to myself that this time it would be different. After all, she was a completely different woman, and she was a mother herself with three children of her own, and once again, I had met her in church. Maybe since I met her in a different church, God would give me a different outcome. Perhaps the marriage would be different because she came from a different culture. Finally, this marriage had to work because we had both grown up in the church, right? Now, I have a title as an elder, so my church title would get us through the tough times, and because I could lead in our church, it definitely meant that I could lead as a husband, father, and stepfather, correct? I had it in the bag.

But if that was the case, why am I here in Massachusetts, by myself, looking in this mirror with tears in my eyes and thoughts of overwhelming shame, regret, and failure? What will my family think? Do my children think I am a loser? What will my church community think of me? Will I ever be able to minister again with integrity? Will my reputation be Gregory Bloomfield, the man who can't keep a woman?

Gentlemen, many of you have had similar thoughts about yourself. You might have failed in something and the guilt is killing you. You could have failed in marriage, with your children, and given up on your dreams. You might have made one wrong move or one bad decision, and it caused you to spend some time in prison, ruin your marriage, or even think about taking your own life or using alcohol, drugs, sex, or other vices to numb the pain. Well, you are not alone, and this book is for you.

I want to introduce what changed my whole life: a spiritual awakening. It was no longer being that guy in church holding on to my religious heritage and traditions, thinking that would make me a good Christian man. It was, and still is, actually becoming a Christian, regardless of titles or church attendance or by relying on my own reputation.

Now, you don't have to be a Christian to read this book. And if you identify as another religion or if you are agnostic or atheist, that's fine. This book is for everybody. That is why I opened my heart and shared my deep failures at the beginning of this introduction. I want to let you know that even church guys like me have some profound shortcomings, but here is the good news: **You might have failed, but you are not a failure.**

After I looked into the mirror, I wanted to change and become a better man—not for a woman, not to reconcile my marriage, and not even for my church family, mother, children, or siblings. This change was for me! I did some reading, and I came across a scripture in the Bible. Galatians 5:22-23 (NKJV) says, "But the Fruit of the Spirit is love, joy, peace, long-suffering, kindness, goodness, faithfulness, gentleness, self-control. Against such there is no law."[1] And it dawned on me that these nine characteristics are what any man needs to be a true man. I also realized that these characteristics and attributes exemplify how Christ is, and if He is a man and if I identify as a Christian, then these are the traits I have as a Christian man. Your church affiliation, title, or even how long you have been in the church don't make you who you are. You don't even have to be a card-carrying believer and you can still have some of these

---

1 Galatians 5:22-23 (NKJV)

traits, but their sources come from God Himself through his Son, Jesus Christ. This is how the 5:22 Man concept was born, from these verses in Galatians chapter 5.

This book is designed for the man who wants to change, be authentic and be a blessing to himself, his spouse, his children, his community, his culture, his church, his country, and this world. Young or old, black or white, rich or poor, churched or unchurched, we can all be a 5:22 Man. Thank you for experiencing this journey with me. Let's get it!

CHAPTER 1

Love

-------⊗≫-------

The Most Overused Word in History

One of the last gifts I gave my second wife before our split was front-row tickets to see our favorite neo-soul singer, Musiq Soulchild. We both loved Musiq's music long before we knew that either of us existed. It was one of the things that we had in common and why we fell for each other. When we left our home and went to the venue where Musiq was performing in Rhode Island, I remember saying to my then wife, "These are the songs that I know he has to sing." She emphatically agreed and even added her own "request list" to the mix. Guess what? Musiq performed the song that was at the top of both of our lists. You may have heard it; it's called "LOVE." The chorus is what most people know from the song:

> Love
> So many people use your name in vain
> Love
> Those who have faith in you sometimes go astray
> Love
> Through all the ups and downs, the joy and hurt
> Love
> For better or worse, I still will choose you first[2]

---

2 Musiq Soulchild, Taalib Johnson, Andre Harris, Carvin Haggins, "Love," Aijuswanaseing, Track #7, Luvan Musiq Publishing, Nivrac Tyke Music, Dirty Dre

Even after the marriage ended, this is still one of my favorite songs because there is so much truth to it, especially the first part of the chorus. So many people use the word *love* in vain. In fact, how do you even define love?

As men in this culture, we use the word *love* for things and people that cannot even love us back. "I love my car," "I love my house," "I love my job," "I love my fans," "I love my dogs (4-legged and 2-legged)." We even confuse love with lust all the time, especially when we are trying to have sexual relations with a woman. How often have you said, "I love you, girl," and you really didn't mean it? Or were you confused with lust and not love? Hey, don't feel bad; I have done it once or twice. (I told you that I am going to be real and honest in this book.) But the conflict is this: in our journey together to become a 5:22 Man, how should we really define love? Is there another way to define and use love to improve ourselves as men?

Redefining Love

I love to go to the dictionary for definitions, and throughout this book, you will find many dictionary definitions for the nine 5:22 Man characteristics. We will begin with love and then apply the proper definitions and examples to help us in our 5:22 journey.

The *Merriam-Webster* dictionary gives us several definitions of *love*. In some cases, *love* is classified as a noun, while in others, it is a verb. Now, if you have completed some level of elementary school education, then you must know the difference between a noun and a verb. A noun is a person, place, or thing. A verb is an action word,

Music, Jat Cat Music Publishing, EMI April Music & Universal Music Group. 2000 whether transitive or intransitive. Some definitions of love as a noun are as follows:[3]

- A strong affection for another arising out of kinship or personal ties.
- An attraction based upon sexual desire.
- An affection based on admiration, benevolence, or common interest.

All these definitions are based on feelings and emotions. Now, every man has feelings and emotions. No matter how hard they try to suppress them or deny that they are there, believe me, brother, they are there inside of you. It is in our best interest as men to accept that and acknowledge that we have emotions and feelings of love for many people, places, and things.

However, for the 5:22 Man, love must also be a verb and an action. Look at *Merriam-Webster*'s definition of *love* when used as a verb:[4]

- To hold dear
- To desire actively
- To thrive in

These are all actions, and I don't know about you, but I like to be active and do things rather than just feel things. Our feelings as men should galvanize us to action. Therefore, when it comes to love for the 5:22 Man, it is a verb and is no longer just a noun or a feeling.

---

3 Merriam-Webster Dictionary, "Love," https://www.merriam-webster.com/dictionary/love.

4 Merriam-Webster Dictionary, "Love," https://www.merriam-webster.com/dictionary/love

Some synonyms for the word love are *adore* and *value*.[5] I believe that is the perfect blend of emotions and actions when we love. Because I adore something or someone, I will treat that thing or that person with value, which means I will actively take part in protecting it and cherishing it because I adore that thing or person. It is very much the basis of how God loves us.

Jesus Is Love

I am a huge music fan, if you don't already know from the beginning of this chapter. In fact, I have played the saxophone since I was a kid, and I dabble a bit with the piano, the drums, and even the flute. I can sing a bit, not lead, but I would be a strong background singer in a men's quartet. But I digress. In seeing the heading "Jesus Is Love," I am reminded of the Commodores song from the '70s. Why do I like this song? Because it is very true. Jesus is Love, and since we are studying His attributes so we can be 5:22 Men, let us look at His love.

We all know this scripture. Even if you are not a Christian or did not grow up in church, most of us know what John 3:16 says: "For God so loved the world that He gave His only begotten Son, that whoever believes in Him should not perish but have everlasting life."[6] Let's unpack this for a minute.

Notice the adoration and the value that God has for us. "For God so loved the world." Now, if you are a part of the world's population, regardless of your country, then, my brother, you are included in God's adoration, and He sees the value in you. But God doesn't just

---

5 Ibid.
6 John 3:16 (NKJV)

stop there. Because of His adoration for you and the value He sees in you, the text says, "He gave." Love from the 5:22 Man will always be a giving and sacrificial response. It will take care of its own, and it will also have considerable value for itself. What exactly did God give? The text says that He gave His own begotten Son. His name is Jesus. Because God loves you so much, He gave up His Son to die in your place. Isn't that the essence of the Christian message? That essence is Love in action, love as a verb.

As 5:22 Men, we must understand that we don't just love through emotion, but we also love in action. 1 John 3:16 says it like this: "By this, we know love because He laid down His life for us. And we also ought to lay down our lives for the brethren."[7] Does that mean that we should literally lay down our lives for people in all situations? Of course, not literally; the point is that we as men should have the same self-sacrificing love (in action) for the people that we are sworn to protect and provide for. The first step is to love God and His sacrifice; the next step is to love yourself.

You Are Loved, So Learn to Love Yourself

As I mentioned in my introduction, I had to reconcile that God still loved me despite my marriage failures, horrible decisions, and mistakes along the way. My mistakes are not my essence. They were just part of the journey. God loves me (adored me and valued me) regardless of what I have done because His Son paid it all on Calvary. And because of His great love for me, I can walk with my head up, not in an arrogant way, but in a confident way because I know that the Father loves me.

---

7 1 John 3:16 (NKJV)

"What is man that You are mindful of him, and the son of man that you visit Him? For You have made him a little lower than the angels. And you have crowned Him with glory and honor."[8]

Even the angels asked God, "What is it about that guy . . . meaning you, brother . . . that you are so fond of him?" God replies, "I adore him, and I value him." My dear brother, regardless of what you have done, you can begin again, and it starts with loving yourself because the Almighty adores and values you. So get up from being down and try again. If you fail, that doesn't change how He feels about you. Learn from the experience and try again. There is no future in your past, so stop looking backward and press forward to your God-given calling. And remember to always walk with your head up because the God of the Universe adores and values you.

Spread the Love

Because you love yourself with a healthy love (which could otherwise be called *self-esteem*), you need to spread that love wherever you go, and it should reflect in what you do. As a 5:22 Man, you must be impactful in all areas of your life. When you love yourself because God loves you, then you can be a better husband, a better father, a better employee, a better employer, a better friend, a better mentor, a better community leader, an honest Christian, and a better overall human being because God's love through Jesus Christ is living in you. It is more profound than just church attendance; it is solely based on a change in your mind and heart.

My fellow 5:22 Man, I celebrate you for taking the first step in your new journey: accepting the love of God in your heart, recognizing

---

[8] Psalms 8:4-5 (NKJV)

what He did for you by giving up His only Son, and accepting that love as your own so you can forgive yourself, start again, and love as a verb, not just as an emotion.

Amen.

CHAPTER 2

Joy

---⊗⊗⊗---

The Pursuit of Happiness

I am not a huge movie buff, but there are some films that I can watch repeatedly. One is *The Shawshank Redemption*, another is *Gladiator*, and one of my favorite movies of all time is *The Pursuit of Happiness* with Will Smith and his son Jaden Smith. It is the semi-autobiographical story of a man named Chris Gardner, and it is such a relatable story with a very powerful message.

Chris was on a quest to be a stockbroker to better his life and his family. He took a free internship with the firm Bear Stearns at the time, and amid pursuing his dreams, his wife left him. Then he went through financial ruin, homelessness, and becoming a single father of a five-year-old boy. Along with sleeping in bus terminals and shelters, he wore the same suit daily, studied, cared for his son, and worked (for free) at the investment firm. During this entire ordeal, Chris had to learn to find joy amid his suffering. He eventually got the job and worked for the firm he interned with. His dream came true, and he eventually started his own firm and became a huge philanthropist, giving back to others, especially the shelter that took him in when he was homeless.

Many of you gentlemen have or currently are going through some tough times. Whether it is unemployment, a company falling apart, sickness due to COVID or other health issues, financial crises, family tragedies, divorce, breakups, difficulty with the courts, being a victim of crime, or anything else, many of us have gone through something tragic or are currently in a bad situation. I am here to encourage you, 5:22 Man, that even during your storm, your situations, and the vacillations in this life, know that God is faithful, He is constant, and I promise you . . . He is with you: "And lo, I am with you always, even to the end of this age".[9]

Just Roll with It

Before I became heavily involved in men's ministries at my church and throughout the Southern New England Region, I was a youth leader, and I still do some youth speaking engagements to this day. A young person approached me many years ago and asked me this question: "Elder Gregory, why is life so unfair?" I had to pause because I had asked myself the same question a time or two. My response to this young person might have been a bit blunt, but I did not have a profound answer for him. I told the young person, "Life is so unfair because that's life." That is honestly how I felt: life is unfair because that's life.

As an adult male, I still feel this way to this day. Many of you gentlemen who are developing into 5:22 Men share my sentiments. Have you ever felt that no matter how hard you try in this life, there will always be setbacks that have nothing to do with your ability, skill, or work ethic? Sometimes in this life, the good guys do not finish first; instead, they finish last. There are many other unfair things about this life.

- Why is most of the world's wealth held by a small percentage of the world's population? (LIFE IS NOT FAIR.)

---

9 Matthew 28:20 (NKJV)

- Why do companies that are failing lay off their employees while the CEO does not take a drop in pay? In fact, they get million-dollar performance bonuses and then the company gets bailed out because they are "too big to fail" while that same CEO keeps his private jet. (LIFE IS NOT FAIR.)

- Why is it that at the altar you said you would love this woman through sickness and health, prosperity and adversity, until death do you part, and then within a few years your vows are broken. You never plan on divorce when you get married. You take all the counseling, go to marriage retreats, and do your best, but you still end up divorced and alone. (LIFE IS NOT FAIR.)

- Why is it that you can work hard at your job, come in on time and always get overlooked for a promotion? Then your coworker who is less qualified than you gets the job because he or she played office politics or did something unethical to get ahead of you (LIFE IS NOT FAIR.)

- Why is it that your child who you love and sacrifice for begins to think he or she is grown and can disrespect or dishonor you with his or her mouth and actions? (LIFE IS NOT FAIR.)

Again, I tell you that life is not fair because it is life. This is why every 5:22 Man should know the difference between happiness and joy.

What Is the Difference Between Happiness and Joy?

You know that I love definitions, and this section is no exception. I went back to the *Merriam-Webster Dictionary* and found this:

Happiness: "a feeling or state of well-being and contentment."[10]

Then I wanted to look up the word *joy*, and I came up with this:

Joy: "the emotion evoked by well-being, success, or good fortune or by the prospect of possessing what one desires."[11]

These definitions are very similar; in some dictionaries, *happiness* and *joy* are synonymous. However, for the first time, I will put my interpretation of happiness and joy, and I do not believe that they are the same. The obvious difference is that joy is a fruit of the Spirit, where happiness is not. Let's go a little bit deeper.

Here is what I believe happiness is:

> *Happiness:* "a sense of pleasure, fulfillment, or contentment due to a situation or event."

For example, if I graduated from college, or if I got a raise at my job, or if I asked a girl to be my girlfriend and she said yes, these would be incidents that give reason to be happy. Let me be clear: There is nothing wrong with being happy. But the 5:22 Man is striving for joy, which can be defined as follows:

Joy: "a sense of peace and contentment regardless of a situation or an event."

That means that regardless of what is going on in my life, I have peace and contentment. That is a fruit of the Spirit or, in other

---

10 Merriam-Webster Dictionary, "Happiness," https://www.merriam-webster.com/dictionary/happiness.
11 Merriam-Webster Dictionary, "Joy," https://www.merriam-webster.com/dictionary/Joy.

words, Christ's characteristic; therefore, as a 5:22 Man in training, we must strive for those traits that mirror Christ.

To contrast, *happiness* comes from the situation, and joy comes from another source other than the situation, which is God. Happiness is temporal, whereas joy is eternal. Happiness can be controlled by other human beings, where joy is given to us by God, and no human being can take it away unless you allow it. In fact, for those of you with a church upbringing, when you were a child and attending either Sabbath school or Sunday school, do you remember that song: "J-O-Y Joy, Joy in the Holy Ghost, Don't let the devil steal your joy"? Did you ever notice that the song is about joy and not happiness? the devil can steal your joy only if you permit him to. That is why I believe that happiness and joy are not the same. We can strive for happiness, but what is more important is that the 5:22 Man persists and keeps his joy.

How Do I Get This Joy?

I am so very happy that you asked this question. I will give five ways that I got my joy back, and my full intention is to keep it, no matter what happens in my life. I am committed to being a 5:22 Man, and joy, along with love, are key ingredients to having this life of victory and power. I want to share those five ways, which come from the Bible. Now I understand that some of you are not Christians, let alone believers. But I want to encourage you that the principles work, and I am speaking from my own personal journey and experience. All I ask is that you have an open mind, and feel free to ask me any other questions after you read these steps.

Step 1 – Allow Jesus to Restore the Joy in Your Heart

> Create in me a clean heart, O God,
>
> And renew a steadfast spirit within me.
>
> Do not cast me away from Your presence,
>
> And do not take Your Holy Spirit from me.
>
> Restore to me the joy of Your salvation,
>
> And uphold me *by Your* generous Spirit.[12]

The first step to obtaining this joy is finding it in Jesus and allowing Him to do the restoration work inside you. Many of you have been disappointed, let down, and discouraged. Many men suffer in silence because we must be everything to everybody. When we don't meet expectations from the job, our spouse, our kids, our church, and our community, it can cause us to become jaded, angry, discouraged, and even depressed. Well, I have good news for you. Jesus cares, and He understands. You can talk to Him, and He will listen to you. He will also give you the power to face these problems and challenges in your life by giving you peace and contentment despite the situation. We earlier defined this as *joy.*

Step 2 – Strive Every Day to Become a 5:22 Man

If we live in the Spirit, let us also walk in the Spirit.[13]

This is a daily walk with Him. You are not going to get it right on the first try, and there may be times when becoming a 5:22 Man in

---

12 Psalms 51:10-13 (NKJV)
13 Galatians 5:25 (NKJV).

all nine areas is extremely challenging and demanding. But that is why we must live in the Spirit of God every day. How? By accepting Jesus and allowing His Spirit to live inside of you. When the Spirit lives inside of you, He gives you that small voice via your conscience to tell you, do this, do not do this, do not do that. He will guide you and give you the free will to listen and choose for yourself. Every man needs accountability and a mentor. Some incredible men tell me when I am right and wrong. These men encourage and celebrate me and chasten and correct me. That is also who the Holy Spirit is for us: our personal accountability partner who lives inside us if we let Him in.

Returning to my original point about the differences between happiness and joy: You don't need God in your life to be happy. Some Christians might get mad at me for saying that, but it is true. You don't need God to be happy! I know plenty of atheists and agnostics who are very happy people without God. However, without God, you will never know precisely what true joy is based on my earlier definition. Take two happy people; one has their wealth and possessions as their source, and the other has a relationship with God. Let tragedy strike for them both. The one without God may turn to drugs, alcohol, and other things to numb the pain, or even have thoughts of suicide. But the one with God in their life should realize that He is still on the throne, that he is not a mistake, and that this is part of a bigger plan from the God of the Universe. There is peace and calm despite his tears and his loss. Gentlemen, happiness will not always travel with you wherever you go, but joy can come along for the ride no matter where you are or who you are with because joy comes from a relationship with God, not a religious experience.

People can repossess your car, your house, or other possessions. Your boss can lay you off, your wife can leave you, and your kids can ignore you, but despite all of this, NEVER let anyone or anything take away your joy. I guarantee you that you will not be happy in those situations, but know that weeping endures for a night, and real 5:22 Men know that joy will always come in the morning. Let's strive for joy through a relationship with God rather than just merely being religious and pious.

Step 3 – Experience God's Sabbath Rest

If you turn away your foot from the Sabbath,

From doing your pleasure on My holy day,

And call the Sabbath a delight,

The holy *day* of the LORD honorable,

And shall honor Him, not doing your own ways,

Nor finding your own pleasure,

Nor speaking *your own* words,

[14] Then you shall delight yourself in the LORD;

And I will cause you to ride on the high hills of the earth,

And feed you with the heritage of Jacob your father.

The mouth of the LORD has spoken.[14]

Some of you are thinking, "Of course you say this, because you are a Sabbath-keeping Christian." Yes, I am a Seventh-Day Adventist,

---

14 Isaiah 58:13-14 (NKJV)

but these principles held true long before there was ever such a thing as a Seventh-Day Adventist. God's principles are not limited to a Christian denomination; they are universal. I believe that to get the joy of the Lord, it is essential to do what the Lord commands. He promises blessings when we delight ourselves in the Lord and honor His Sabbath. Now, most Christian theologians will agree that the Sabbath is Friday sundown to Saturday sundown. My tradition and my family tradition is that I do not do any secular work during that time, and I use that time to fellowship with my church family, to pray and worship and make it a God-focused day. It is my way of having a relationship with God and making quality time for Him. It doesn't mean I only do this on the Sabbath; I make time for God daily. But on the Sabbath, I rest from work, focus on God, and show thankfulness toward Him.

Now, if you are one of my Christian friends who goes to church on Sunday, I say, "Praise the Lord for you!" The most important thing is that you love Jesus. But I want to challenge the 5:22 Men out there to add the Sabbath into your 5:22 experience and experience His rest, His joy, and His blessings. I could do a whole book on this topic, but all I can say is try it. God says that He will cause us to ride on the high hills of the Earth, which means blessings and favor. The 5:22 Man will experience the joy of God by making quality time and special time on the day that He said we should observe. This is not just an Old Testament thing. This is also relevant in the New Testament and for people today. Read Hebrews 4:8-10 and give the Sabbath a try.

Step 4 – Enter into a Life of Service to Others

If you seek joy in your life, then as a 5:22 Man, you must find purpose in your life that cannot just be found in a job or worldly possessions. In fact, Sir Wilfred T. Grenfell, the great British medical missionary, said the following, "The service we render to others is really the rent we pay for our room on this earth. It is obvious that man is himself a traveler; that the purpose of this world is not 'to have and to hold' but to 'give and serve.' There can be no other meaning."[15] In my opinion, this is true joy: serving people and being an asset in the world rather than being a liability. In fact, the Bible supports this truth from Mr. Grenfell.

If you read Matthew 25:14-30, you will read about the parable of the talents. Many of you already know the story. A master gives one man five talents, another two talents, and another just one. You will see something exciting if you carefully look at verses 20-23:

> And he who had received the five talents came forward, bringing five talents more, saying, "Master, you delivered to me five talents; here, I have made five talents more." His master said to him, "Well done, good and faithful servant. You have been faithful over a little; I will set you over much. Enter into the joy of your master." And he also who had the two talents came forward, saying, "Master, you delivered to me two talents; here, I have made two talents more." His master said to him, "Well done, good and faithful servant. You have been faithful over a little; I will set you over much. Enter into the joy of your master."[16]

---

15 Steve Ward, "Finding Purpose by Serving Others," lifeimprovementsteps.com.
16 Matthew 25:20-23 (ESV)

Did you see it? The master tells the man with the five talents and the man with the two talents to enter into the *joy* of their master. Notice it is not the *happiness* of the master, but rather the *joy* of the master. This lets us know that there is joy in sowing and serving. Why is that? It is straightforward: All of us have problems and challenges. Joy allows you to realize that some people in this world have it much worse than you. So when we encourage, sow, and serve into their lives, God, who is the great master in this parable, will cause us to enter into His joy. And when you join His joy, you allow Him to have his way in your life. In other words, if you take care of others and serve your wife, kids, community, and others, you better believe that God will take care of your issues and problems on the back end. Glory to God! So the best way to have joy is to serve.

Hopefully, these four different steps will help you obtain the joy of the Lord as you continue to cultivate your love for Him and mirror Christ's characteristics as we walk in this 5:22 Man journey together!

Amen!

CHAPTER 3

Peace

———— ⬡ ————

The older I get, the more beautiful the word *peace* becomes to me. It is one of my favorite attributes, as I am striving to become a 5:22 Man. (I am not there yet, so that is why I must read my own book from time to time.)

When people say the word *peace*, they define it many ways. Some of those definitions or synonyms for *peace* could be as follows:

- To be quiet
- To be tranquil
- Freedom from disturbance
- Lack of oppressive thoughts or feelings
- Harmonious relationships
- Time without war
- Absence of hostility or harm

In the *Merriam-Webster Dictionary*, there are several definitions for peace. Two that jump out to me are the ones that describe peace as a noun:[17]

---

17 Merriam-Webster Dictionary, "Peace," https://www.merriam-webster.com/dictionary/peace.

- A state of tranquility or quiet, such as freedom from civil disturbance or a state of security or order within a community provided for by law or custom.

- A state or period of harmony in personal relations or between governments.

While the standard and official dictionary definitions are not incorrect, I believe they are from a viewpoint that doesn't include God in the equation. The world's peace is inferior to God's peace, and as a 5:22 Man in training, this is the peace that we must go after. Like the differences between happiness and joy discussed in the previous chapter, worldly peace is temporary. It is dependent on the circumstances developed and allowed by human beings. Divine peace exists despite the circumstances human beings will throw at us. When things are calm, we have Divine peace; when things in our life grow dim, we can still have that Divine peace. You may say to me, "Gregory, you have no idea what I have been through in my life." Do you know what? You are right; I could never imagine what you have been through, or maybe I could because I have been through it myself. I acknowledge your pain and frustration. However, my brother, hold on! I am here to encourage you that Divine peace may seem beyond your comprehension, but it is not beyond your grasp.

Allow me to repeat myself: Divine peace may seem beyond your comprehension, but it is not beyond your grasp. This real peace is readily available to you and to me. Here is how in four steps.

Four Steps to Divine Peace
Step #1 – Find Peace *with* God

I believe the first step to finding peace *with* God is to find it through His Son, Jesus Christ. Now, I know what some of you are thinking: "Of course you will say this, because you are a Christian." You are right. I am a Christian. No false advertising here. But I do realize something about us as men. Regardless of a man's religious persuasion and beliefs, or lack of them, every man wants and needs to find purpose in their life, and most importantly, a man *needs* peace. This peace must be present and consistent in all areas of life, especially in his mind, his relationship with his spouse (or significant other), and his home. As men, we can accept chaos on the job to a certain extent, but I have yet to meet a man who does not want peace in the three areas I just mentioned. If these three areas do not have peace, you may end up with a shell of a man. Trust me. I know what I am talking about and can relate to you, my brother. I had the dubious experience of being a shell of a man for most of my previous marriage in all three peace points mentioned above. There were times when I almost felt suicidal based on how empty I felt, and that was because of the lack of peace in my mind, my relationship with my spouse, and my home. Every man is searching for that peace, and there are many paths that a man can take to find that peace. I found that path through Jesus Christ, my Lord and Savior. And when I chose to become more accepting of His peace, His Love, and His Joy, those things, among others, gave me Divine peace, despite what I was experiencing in my marriage or any other adverse circumstance I was going through. So I can only talk about what I know and have experienced. No shade toward any other man's beliefs, but I know that Jesus and the Christian faith have worked personally for me, and that is what I want to share with you. True peace comes from God through His son Jesus Christ. Why don't you give Him a try today?

Romans 5:1 says the following, "Therefore, since we have been justified [that is, acquitted of sin, declared blameless before God] by faith, [let us grasp the fact that] we have peace with God [and the joy of reconciliation with Him] through our Lord Jesus Christ (the Messiah, the Anointed)."[18]

Jesus has declared you blameless before God, which means no matter what you have done and the shame of your past, He has come before God on your behalf, and God has declared you "not guilty"! But you must believe that you are not guilty, which is why the verse says "by faith" you have been declared not guilty in the eyes of God, and now you can have access to the heavenly and divine mindset and His peace, knowing that you are fully acquitted of your mistakes. That is why I love the Christian faith. Jesus paid it all on my behalf, and this verse has reconciled us back to God, which means that we are His children and have access to what He has through His son, Jesus Christ. Doesn't that give you peace? Isn't that a good feeling? All you have to do is accept your part in the mistake (which is accountability), say that you are sorry to God (and, if you can, to those whom you hurt), turn from your mistakes (which is repentance), and accept that you are forgiven. And from there, you can have peace with God, and you are on your way to becoming a true 5:22 Man. Find peace with God, my brother. It is available to you today, right here and right now.

---

18 Romans 5:1 (AMP)

Step #2 – Experience the Peace *of* God

It is possible to make the peace of God your consistent reality in these modern days. Let's look at another verse in the book of Romans. This time let us look at Romans 8:6-11 and the passage of scripture gives us the difference between the worldly mind and the Spirit-controlled mind.

Now the mind of the flesh is death [both now and forever—because it pursues sin]; but the mind of the Spirit is life and peace [the spiritual well-being that comes from walking with God—both now and forever]; the mind of the flesh [with its sinful pursuits] is actively hostile to God. It does not submit itself to God's law since it cannot, and those who are in the flesh [living a life that caters to sinful appetites and impulses] cannot please God.

However, you are not [living] in the flesh [controlled by the sinful nature] but in the Spirit, if, in fact, the Spirit of God lives in you [directing and guiding you]. But if anyone does not have the Spirit of Christ, he does not belong to Him [and is not a child of God]. If Christ lives in you, though your [natural] body is dead because of sin, your spirit is alive because of righteousness [which He provides]. And if the Spirit of Him who raised Jesus from the dead lives in you, He who raised Christ Jesus from the dead will also give life to your mortal bodies through His Spirit, who lives in you.[19]

This passage of Scripture indeed shows us the following contrast:

Worldly mind = no peace.

Spirit-controlled mind (or the 5:22 Man) = Divine peace.

---

19 Romans 8:6-11 (AMP)

When we as men continually entertain thoughts that are not good for us spiritually and rely on the culture to define us as men, we will move further away from what God wants us to be and have. A man will never have the peace of God when he surrenders to his vices and sinful nature. They are warring against each other. It is like oil and water; they cannot coexist. However, when we bring ourselves under subjection by surrendering to God and obtaining His peace, we will be at Divine peace because the Greater One is within us. You will have peace when you walk and when you talk. Peace will exude your very being so that people won't even see you; they will see the God in you because you reflect Christ's character . . . this is the 5:22 Man!

Philippians 4:6-7 says, "Be anxious for nothing, but in everything by prayer and supplication, with thanksgiving, let your requests be made known to God; and the PEACE OF GOD, which surpasses all understanding, will guard your hearts and minds through Christ Jesus."[20]

The 5:22 Man experiences the peace of God through his time with God and having conversations with him through prayer. When he is facing problems, he goes to his peace source, God, for compassion, strength, wisdom, and strategies to handle that situation. The young 5:22 Man will pray during his studies to seek compassion, strength, wisdom, and strategy to handle that huge term paper, that assignment, that training program, and even who to date as he is looking for his wife and life partner. A 5:22 Man is a praying man. He also supplicates, which means to pray and intercede for others. A 5:22 Man not only prays for himself but also

---

20 Philippians 4:6-7 (NKJV)

goes to the Father to cover his wife (or significant other if he is unmarried). He will also ask for compassion, strength, wisdom, and strategies to be a good husband and covering for his marriage. The 5:22 Man will pray for his children and speak life to them. Whether he lives in the home with his children or not, a 5:22 Man is still responsible for presiding, protecting, and providing for them. That is why a 5:22 Man must seek guidance in those areas and supplicate daily for his babies. A 5:22 Man should also supplicate for his family, friends, enemies (we will talk about that in a moment), place of worship, community, employer, employees, and everyone that he can think of.

Finally, a 5:22 Man is a thankful man. He blesses God for the good times and the bad times, when he has it and when he does not have it. Peace does not come from things and possessions. True Divine peace comes from the one living inside you, God, through His son, Jesus Christ. This is how the peace of God will come to you and guard your hearts and minds!

Step #3 – Once You Have This Divine peace . . . *Always* Protect It

The easiest way to have Divine peace is to first have peace *with* God and then follow that by experiencing the peace *of* God. Anytime you take care of your vertical relationship with God, He will help you with your horizontal relationships with other human beings. Once you have this Divine peace, it is up to you to protect the peace you worked hard to obtain. It is so easy to forget this once you have received it. Also, let's face it: people today can truly test your peace. Gentlemen, the people that try our peace the most either work with us or live with us. Do I have a witness? Please remember two things when it comes to protecting your peace: (1) You can protect your peace by blessing others and not cursing them, and (2) you can protect your peace by setting clear boundaries.

When people try to mess up your peace, the culture tells us to hit them back with something worse and mess up their life. Please don't do that. You are a 5:22 Man in training. We move differently now because the Divine peace of God lives in us.

"Bless those who persecute you; bless and do not curse them."[21] As hard as this is to do, you can do it. Trust me, I have failed in this area where I intended to ignore that person, but they were trying me, and my breaking point hit, and then my mouth had no manners. Yup! I didn't curse the person out; I *cussed* the person out! It felt good at the time, but later my conscience bothered me, and I had to apologize. I was not a 5:22 Man in training. Now that I am, I would have handled the situation much differently. I had to learn that any dog can fight, but a 5:22 Man will trust God in all situations and never let anything or anyone destroy his peace *with* God or his peace *in* God.

Continue to read Romans 12:14-21 when you have a chance. One of my favorite parts of that passage is verse 18. "If possible, so far as it depends on you, live *peaceably* with all."[22] The apostle tells us that we should live peaceably with people as much as possible. What is the point of working so hard to get Divine peace with God and within us to not give that same peace to others, particularly those that annoy us? A 5:22 Man will be a peaceful person and will bring Divine peace everywhere that he goes. However, the 5:22 Man is no punk either. Sometimes he must set clear boundaries for those who do not respect his Divine peace or try to challenge it, attack it, or

---

21 Romans 12:14 (NKJV)
22 Romans 12:18 (NKJV)

even ruin it. This is why the second part of peace protection is setting up clear boundaries.

Look at Romans 12:18 again. Apostle Paul reminds us that some people will not want to operate in peace. Why? Because likely there is no peace in them, or their peace is worldly or based on the culture and not Divine. Some people in this world love drama, stress, and strife. That is not me anymore.

Have you ever received a call and seen the number on your phone and asked yourself the following questions before you even picked up the call:

- Why are you calling me?
- Why are you even here in my life?
- What drama is this person bringing to me now?

The older I get, the more I realize I can love people from a distance. In fact, that is the only way that you can genuinely stay sane. If you respond to every comment, whether verbal or on social media, you will go crazy, and you will lose your Divine peace. Sometimes you need a break from the phone, the computer, social media, and even from friends, acquaintances, and some family members to protect your peace! Brother, never apologize for protecting your sanity and your mental health. *Never!* Set the boundary, whether permanent or temporary, and keep on living. Some friendships may have to end to protect your peace. I have had to learn on my journey that just because someone is no longer my friend does not mean that you are my enemy. Not all human relationships are salvageable. Some have a Divine expiration date. Accept it and move on with your Divine peace because you have protected it!

Step 4 – Understand That Peace Does Not Equal Perfection

Now that you have become a 5:22 Man in training and experienced the gift of salvation, which is the genesis of your peace with God, know that there will be some disappointing days ahead. You will continue to see the imperfections in this world, starting with you. I heard a pastor once say, "If I'm going to live at peace, then I must surrender my expectation of perfection. Peace isn't found in a place or in a set of circumstances that are problem-free." I really had to think about this, and the pastor was correct. It is the tests in this life that create the character we want to exhibit. If you strive to be a 5:22 Man, you must be tested. Good athletes must be tested to prove they are the best in their sport. So why would it not be any different in your walk with Christ and your 5:22 journey?

Embrace the challenges that God will allow you to undertake. Your peace will be tested. Your coworker will do something to betray you. Your kids will say something disrespectful to you. Your wife may have slick words toward you. Someone may cut you off on the highway, and you will want to curse them out. These things are all trials and tests of your new walk with Christ. You can be an overcomer and keep the peace you have worked hard to obtain.

You got this! Remember, Jesus said, "I have said these things to you, that in me you may have peace. In the world you will have tribulation. But take heart; I have overcome the world."[23]

A 5:22 Man has Divine peace! Obtain it, and always protect it!

Amen.

---

23 John 16:33 (NKJV)

CHAPTER 4

Longsuffering

———⊷⊷———

This part of the book was the most difficult to write. Let me just cut to the chase: I struggle in this area, as I am not the most long-suffering person in the world. So as I was writing this book, in my head, I was saying, "Bloomfield, you better read this chapter every day after the book comes out because this truly isn't you." And do you know what? My head is correct. Being long-suffering, or patient, is not a strong suit. Many of you gentlemen can share the same testimony as me. But that is why we are working on becoming 5:22 Men. One of Jesus's greatest attributes was His patience. If we intend to move from just existing in the world as a man to living as a 5:22 Man, then we need to develop our long-suffering attributes.

Our good friends at *Merriam-Webster Dictionary* define *long-suffering* as "patiently enduring lasting or hardship."[24] This is the absolute antithesis of modern culture today. Very few people want to be patient and wish to endure anything, especially when it comes to hardship or suffering. A good friend said we live in a "microwave society." Everything must be instant, fast, and quick. From food to transportation, even waiting in line at the grocery store, event, or social gathering, no one likes to wait on things. This is how the world is today. We are all in a rush, and many of us lack patience. Many of us, when we are somewhere and see a set of stairs and

---

24 Merriam-Webster Dictionary, "Peace," https://www.merriam-webster.com/dictionary/long-suffering.

beside it an escalator, would instead take the escalator. But because of our society and how being impatient is embedded in the modern North American culture, we now subconsciously walk up the escalator because it is moving too slowly.

Prayer Is a Dangerous Thing!

Growing up in church most of my life, I was always told to pray about everything. Never worry and give everything to God; He will answer your prayers during your due season. I still believe that to a certain extent. In my life's journey and seeing the spiritual life of others and their journeys, I noticed that prayer is a dangerous thing. Not just for the person you are praying for or interceding for, but for yourself. Let me give you an example: My brother, if you are praying to God and asking Him to cure you of your temper, then do you clearly understand what you are asking Him to do? You are asking Him to send people your way to quite literally tick you off, and you are asking God to help you not react to this. You are asking God to send people on the road to cut you off on the highway and then flip you the bird, so you can then wave to that person and say, "Praise the Lord, God Bless you," at the red light. Most of you would cuss them back, flip them your middle finger, and keep it moving. That has been me—even on the way to church. Yup! I've done it (and you probably have too).

Let me give you another example. When you pray to God to learn how to love as He loves, do you know what you are asking for? You are asking the Lord to sign you up for people to hurt you . . . unintentionally and intentionally. Then, after they hurt you and break your heart, turn around, forgive them, and treat them better than before that person committed the offense against you. Do you see my point in these two examples? Sometimes, we don't understand what we ask when we pray. I am not saying that you should not pray like this, not at all. I am saying that whenever we wish to make character changes in our lives, there will be struggle and pain. How can you overcome a problem until you face it head-on and conquer it with the help of the Holy Spirit living inside us? Therefore, as a 5:22 Man in training, you are signing up for a challenging journey. Nobody has ever made a radical change in their life or the world without having to go through sacrifice and face their flaws head-on. It is the same thing with long-suffering and patience.

When you ask God for long-suffering or patience in whatever area of your life you are lacking, do you understand what you are asking God for? You are asking God to allow you to endure long-term hardship or discomfort, so you can then learn to not complain about it. This is the challenge. Are you ready for this in your 5:22 Man training?

I Missed the Bus

I grew up in Toronto, Canada, for the first twenty-three years of my life. I was born in Parkdale, but my mom moved us up to North York, where she bought her first house in her early thirties. I do not usually speak about this, but I was tested to be gifted in grade three and sent to schools outside of my district with an academically gifted program. First, it was Seneca Hill Public School, then Zion Heights Middle School, and then Earl Haig Secondary School (in the US, that would be a high school). At Earl Haig, there was a school of the arts named Claude Watson School of the Arts, of which I took music as an elective. I played saxophone in the jazz band and still play to this day. One day, I might finally put an album out (from my lips to God's ears).

Anyway, one of the perks of being in the gifted program in Toronto was that you get free public transportation. The school provided me with bus and train tickets for three because I had to travel on two buses to get to school, which on a good day would take about forty minutes one way. I was running a little late and had to be at school at a particular time for a meeting before classes started. It was winter, and I ran to the bus stop. The bus was pulling up to my stop, Sheppard East 85E. The E stood for Express, which meant I could get to my meeting early or on time. I hate being late for most things. I was near the stop, and then the driver looked at me, then looked at the road, and then drove away because his light was green. He didn't stop for the kid with a saxophone case and a school bag over his two shoulders (that would be me). Man, I was angry, upset, and developing great impatience for the next bus. I remember I cursed and swore *loudly*. "That bus driver was racist!" I said aloud. And he wasn't even White. That was how irrational I was.

So now here I was, at the bus stop. I was waiting for the next express bus to come, but another Sheppard East 85E was not coming for another fifteen to twenty minutes. However, a Sheppard East 85, with no E, pulled up within five minutes of my tirade. Too bad it was a local bus which made every stop. I thought I was too good for the local bus, but I had to get on it to get to the meeting, for which I was going to be late. I put my free bus ticket in the box, took my transfer, sat near the back of the bus, and was *mad!* Why didn't that first bus driver stop for me? Didn't he know that I had an important meeting? After all, this was Earl Haig Secondary School, and I was in the academically gifted program. Can't you tell? Don't you know my name? My name is Gregory Bloomfield. Every express bus named Sheppard East 85E must stop for me! Yup. I was that full of myself in high school.

I saw something while traveling with the commoners on the Sheppard East 85 local bus (with no E) to my school. I noticed that traffic was slowing down. Of course, I got even more upset because of my appointment, and , I was on a local bus, and the local bus was too slow. At this moment, I thought about getting off the bus and walking to school—all eight to ten miles. Yes, I was this irrational. But then I stayed on the bus and saw the reason for the traffic. That express bus I missed had gotten into a terrible accident with another car that ran a light. Everyone stared at the accident; this was what caused the delay. After we passed the scene of the accident, traffic freed up. If I had made the express bus, I could have been involved in that accident while on the bus, and I would have never made it to school at all. Missing the express bus could have saved my life. Yes, getting on the local bus made me late for the meeting, but guess what? I am alive today to tell you about this story, and God knew in the distant future that He wanted me to tell this story in a book called *The 5:22 Man* to teach other men, including me, that patience and long-suffering are good things and can save your life.

Patience Is a Good Thing

I shared my high school testimony to show you that long-suffering is a good thing, and God allows us, as 5:22 Men in training, to develop this attribute to trust Him and to build our character behind the scenes. Patience is a blessing.

The Canadian-born French tennis player Mary Pierce said something very interesting about patience: "Sometimes things aren't clear right away. That's where you need to be patient and persevere and see where things lead."[25]

When things do not go my way, it becomes uncomfortable and annoying. Especially when you have a plan and some unforeseen factor messes up that plan. Or someone, often who you trusted to execute a task that you depended on for success, lets you down. Also, there are times when we let ourselves down in life with a wrong decision, a bad choice, or even a bad habit or proclivity. There are many things in this life that we cannot control as much as things that we can (that is the topic in chapter 9). But I am here to encourage you, as a 5:22 Man in training, to ask God to give you the strength to be patient and let God move that mountain for you.

One of my favorite scriptures in this area can be found in Romans 5:3-5:[26]

And not only *this* but [with joy] let us exult in our sufferings *and* rejoice in our hardships, knowing that hardship (distress, pressure, trouble) produces patient endurance; and endurance, proven character (spiritual maturity); and proven character, hope *and* confident assurance [of eternal salvation]. Such hope [in God's promises] never disappoints *us* because God's love has been abundantly poured out within our hearts through the Holy Spirit who was given to us.

I love this scripture in the Amplified Version of the Bible because it truly lays out why patience and long-suffering are good for the 5:22 Man, not bad. Notice the scripture says that we should exult in our

---

25 Emma Taubenfeld, "25 Patience Quotes That Inspire Peaceful Persistence," Readers Digest, Last modified Feb 18, 2022, www.rd.com/list/patience-quotes.
26 Romans 5:3-5 (AMP)

suffering. *Exult* is another way of saying be "extremely joyful."[27] So the Apostle Paul tells us that we should be extremely joyful (not happy; go back and read the chapter on joy) and rejoice in our hardships. That is what I call *counterculture.* The 5:22 Man is not a common man but a man that is countering culture. He is unique. He is different. He doesn't react or act like every other man. Why? Because he has 5:22 attributes in him, which mirror the character of Christ. We should praise God, have joy, and rejoice when we go through hard times. It does not mean that we don't have concerns or that we aren't scared at times, but we know that this test or trial is an opportunity for God to show up and show out in the life of the 5:22 Man and the lives of everyone connected to him. Glory to God!

Our sufferings that we go through can be a direct plan from God for character development and perfection within our 5:22 journey. The verse gives us four traits that hard times develop in us if we allow it: patient endurance, character, and hope and confident assurance. All three of these traits are embedded in the 5:22 Man. A man that has patience is a 5:22 Man. A man that can endure challenging times is a 5:22 Man. A man with integrity and character lives his life with morals and codes, that is a 5:22 Man. A man with hope in a Divine power bigger than himself is a 5:22 Man. A man that has confidence in himself because the Spirit of God lives within him is a 5:22 Man. A man with the unwavering assurance that no matter what problems he faces, God will always guide him amid all storms no matter what problems he faces, that is a 5:22 Man. To my gentlemen reading this book, long-suffering is a great blessing and

---

27 Merriam-Webster Dictionary, "Exult," https://www.merriam-webster.com/dictionary/exult.

is necessary to be a 5:22 Man—a man of character and distinction for the service and the kingdom of the Almighty God.

So I encourage you, my brother, to pray to God for the wonderful attribute of patience. Not just for situations, not just for your spouse, kids, job, business, team, church, or even friends. But also, have patience for yourself. You may sometimes get it wrong, brothers. And that's okay. Keep at it. Keep working on the 5:22 plan. Keep striving for greatness in God. Keep serving God, and this patience and long-suffering will pay off. The Genevan philosopher, writer, and composer Jean-Jacques Rousseau said, "Patience is bitter, but its fruit is sweet."[28] The Catholic bishop Francis De Sales said, "Have patience with all things but first of all with yourself."[29] But I like the way the prophet Isaiah said it in the Bible. Isaiah said, "Those that wait upon the Lord (hallelujah) shall renew their strength. They shall mount up with wings like eagles. They shall run and not be weary. They shall walk and not faint."[30]

My brother, let's learn to be long-suffering, for there is a blessing in the end when we are patient.

Amen!

---

28 Emma Taubenfeld, "25 Patience Quotes That Inspire Peaceful Persistence," Readers Digest, Last modified Feb 18, 2022, www.rd.com/list/patience-quotes.
29 Ibid.
30 Isaiah 40:31 (NKJV)

CHAPTER 5

Kindness

———⊱❈⊰———

I had the distinct privilege of hearing the late Maya Angelou give a commencement speech at my older cousin's graduation from her doctorate degree at Virginia Commonwealth University (VCU) many years ago. At that time, I had never seen so many lights flashing before and after a speech in my life. I have always admired her literary work and how she was a Black woman with so much strength, courage, and grace. She had so many quotable moments, but I want to share with you two of them that tie into our following 5:22 Man's attribute: kindness.

Ms. Angelou said the following:

I think we all have empathy. We may not have enough courage to display it.[31]

It takes courage to be kind.[32]

I agree with Ms. Angelou.

Kindness is something that is not encouraged in this culture when it comes to men. The culture teaches us to be greedy and selfish and get as much money and material things as possible, to step on anyone who even thinks to do us wrong. We don't discuss our problems as men; we fight or even shoot each other like we are in a

---

31 "88 Best Quotes About Kindness to Make the World Better," GoodGoodGood, Last Modified November 28, 2022, www.goodgoodgood.co/articles/kindness-quotes.
32 Ibid.

video game. I have a special burden in my heart for men that look like me: the Black man.

My Burden for People That Look Like Me

My younger brother is a police officer in Toronto. He has told me many stories about his job and the challenges that come with it. So when I hear about the police and the brutality that exists between them and Black people in the United States, I can genuinely see both sides. From my personal experience, I have also been a victim of being Black and being harassed by the police while I was in high school. I will save that story for another book, but I can understand the rage of that violation from a man with a badge and a gun. To be very transparent, during the George Floyd murder in Minnesota, I had PTSD because it reminded me of my high school violation. I had to speak to my therapist about it in several sessions. So, yes, the problem of police violations against the African American community is real. However, we as Black people must do a much better job within our communities to treat each other better, and it starts with us as Black men.

Check out these statistics from the Federal Bureau of Investigation (FBI). This comes from the 2019 database on murder in the United States, and it explicitly deals with the race of murder victims versus the race and sex of the offender.[33]

In 2019, there was a total percentage breakdown of recorded murders committed by a single offender to a single victim. Of the race of each of these victims:

---

33 "2019 Crime in the United States: Expanded Homicide Data Table 6," Federal Bureau of Investigation, www.ucr.fbi.gov/crime-in-the-u.s./2019/crime-in-the-u.s.-2019/tables/expanded-homicide-data-table-6.xls.

- 50% of the victims were White.
- 44% of the victims were Black.
- 6% of the victims were from Other races.[34]

Of the 44% of the Black murder victims, here is how the race of their offenders breaks down:

- 88.6% of the offenders were Black.
- 8.5% of the offenders were White.
- 3.0% of the offenders were of other races.

And if we break this down by offenders' sex, here are some more staggering statistics:

- 89.7% of the offenders were males.
- 9.4% of the offenders were females.
- 0.9% of the offenders' sex was unknown.

So based on the FBI data presented, if 44% of the murder victims were Black in 2019 and 88.6% of the offenders were Black, and 89.7% of the offenders were male, then it is a safe estimate to say that 79.5% of Black males murdered Black people (both men and women). That is clearly not demonstrative of kindness within the Black community. So if we are going to protest and shout about Black Lives Matter, we need to consistently show that Black Lives Matter within our community and show kindness to one another—quickly, and it starts with us, Black Man!

---

34 Ibid. This would include American Indian or Alaska Native, Asian, Native Hawaiian or Other Pacific Islander, and unknown races.

White Men, You Are Not Much Better

Before I continue with this book, allow me to be perfectly clear. Black-on-Black crime is a real problem in the Black community. Data supports it. However, it does not absolve the fact that there is White on White crime also. White people kill White people. Using the same statistics, check this out for White people, which make up 50% of the total single victim/single offender murders in America in 2019:[35]

- 78.6% of the offenders were White.
- 17.2% of the offenders were Black.
- 4.2% of the offenders were of other races.

And if we break this down by offenders' sex, here are some more staggering statistics:

- 88.4% of the offenders were males.
- 10.9% of the offenders were females.
- 0.8% of the offenders' sex was unknown.

Using the same mathematical logic, this means that 69.5% of White men kill White people (male and female). So even though Black men kill our own at a higher percentage than White people kill their own, to my White brothers, you also have a problem in your community. So before discussing and criticizing the Black community, please fix your community. Thank you.

---

35 "2019 crime in the United States: Expanded Homicide Data Table 6," Federal Bureau of Investigation, www.ucr.fbi.gov/crime-in-the-u.s./2019/crime-in-the-u.s.-2019/tables/expanded-homicide-data-table-6.xls.

Regardless of race, we all, as men, have a kindness problem!

What Does Kindness Look Like?

Instead of looking up the word *kindness* in the dictionary, I looked directly at the thesaurus. Most people can define *kindness* by simply using the word *kind*. The word *kind* can be further defined as an adjective for someone being considerate, thoughtful, or acting in the need of others, usually without being asked. These are all excellent descriptions, but the best way to define kindness is through words that have a similar meaning. These words will help us with our 5:22 Man training. Here are the words per *Merriam-Webster*.[36]

- Benevolence
- Compassion

Benevolence in Action

A 5:22 Man is a benevolent man. That means he makes it a point to do good to those around him, including himself and his family. This is one of the traits of kindness. Benevolence in action is the fact that you want to do the right thing for people and treat people kindly. What I have found in my life is that people who tend to do cruel things to others or inconsiderate things tend not to like themselves. They mask it with money, clothes, and other material things, but deep down inside, that person does not like themselves. When someone truly healthily loves themselves and has knowledge of self and a love for God, they want to pour kindness into the world through their benevolence. That is why the 5:22 Man seeks to be

---

36 Merriam-Webster Dictionary, "Kindness," https://www.merriam-webster.com/thesaurus/kindness.

kind to their fellow man, even if they don't deserve it. Why? Because isn't that what God has done for you?

Ephesians 4:32 says to the 5:22 Man that he should "be kind to one another, tenderhearted, forgiving one another, as God in Christ forgave you."[37]

As Maya Angelou said, it takes courage to be kind. Therefore, as a 5:22 Man, courage is necessary to go against the culture and to be benevolent by caring for the poor without an audience or applause, to volunteer his time and talents without always expecting remuneration, and to sow seeds of love, joy, and peace to others in all situations because someone has been kind to him.

Compassion in Action

A 5:22 Man is a compassionate man. He never wants to add stress to people's lives, but instead, he wants to seek ways to alleviate it in the lives of the people he loves. He shows sympathy to others and is very slow to judge. He walks a mile in someone's shoes before he gives a critique. A 5:22 Man is working on his emotional intelligence, not just his book sense. We live in an era where men want to be more innovative in their trade, earn the most money, be the best providers for their families, and have skill, influence, and a pedigree. But so many of us as men, particularly in our relationships with the opposite sex, have no idea what it is to be compassionate and emotionally intelligent.

There are entire books on emotional intelligence, so I will not go into those details here, but generally, emotional intelligence involves how you manage your emotions, your ability to be self-

---

37 Ephesians 4:32 (ESV)

aware, your social awareness, and how to manage your relationships. The last part is crucial for dealing with your significant other, children, and employees (or clients). My brother, it is not enough for you to pay the bills and be the "head of the house." As a 5:22 Man, you must be the most emotionally intelligent person in your household. As a men's ministry leader for my church and denominational region, I have spoken to many men about a well-known concept for Christian men. We are to protect, provide, and preside (otherwise known as the 3 P's). We, as men, get the first two P's right, but we need to catch up on the preside part. My brother, we don't have to have all the answers, and sometimes, it is just good for us to listen and not try to solve everything. The Bible does give us some tips on how to relate to our spouses, our children, and our employees. Look at Colossians 3, starting at verse 18.

Between verse 18 and Colossians 4:1, it gives the 5:22 Man the blueprint of how he should treat his family and the people close to him. We as men realize that God cares about our human relationships, and God charges us, as men, to treat those relationships with great care. Paul gives not only instruction to the wife, the kids, and your employees (or in those days, they were called *slaves*, which is a word unto itself) but also to the husband, the father, and the employer.

Compassion for Your Wife

Verse 19 says, "Husbands, love your wives [with an affectionate, sympathetic, selfless love that always seeks the best for them] and do not be embittered *or* resentful toward them [because of the responsibilities of marriage]."[38]

The 5:22 Man is called to love his wife and be affectionate, sympathetic, and selfless. It is incredible that some men show more affection and sympathy to their male friends than they do to their wives. I know some men who are more loyal and show greater fidelity to their barber than their spouse. They will hug the woman at church tight and wish them a happy week, but they barely touch their wife in public, and it is worse when they get home. This is out of order! The 5:22 Man is devoted to his wife and puts her as the top priority, one notch below God. The 5:22 Man will listen to his wife's needs and do his best to anticipate them. He will be quick to say he is sorry when he is wrong. When arguments come (and they will), he knows that the goal is not for him to win the argument, but to listen to understand his wife and come to a peaceful solution where everyone can win and the marriage will be blessed.

I told you that one of my favorite singers is Musiq Soulchild, but another of my favorite singers in the neo-soul genre is Eric Roberson. He has a song on one of his older albums called "I'm Not Trying to Keep Score No More."[39] The title of this song says it all. Brother, are you trying to win an argument, or are you trying to continue to win your lady? What is more important to you? If the latter is more important, become a 5:22 Man and learn techniques to boost your emotional intelligence and be compassionate to her, and then you will have no problem with Colossians 3:18 because she will fall in love with you again and again.

---

38 Colossians 3:19 (AMP)

39 Aaron Hardin, Eric Roberson, Zachariah McGant, "I'm Not Trying to Keep Score No More," The Box, Track #3, Blue Erro Soul, August 11, 2014.

Compassion for Your Children

Going back to Colossians 3:21, it says: "Fathers, do not provoke *or* irritate *or* exasperate your children [with demands that are trivial or unreasonable or humiliating or abusive; nor by favoritism or indifference; treat them tenderly with lovingkindness], so they will not lose heart *and* become discouraged *or* unmotivated [with their spirits broken]."[40]

One of the reasons we have so many young people confused, lost, and wanting nothing to do with church or even God is because a father was not compassionate or kind to his children. The 5:22 Man is not that type of father. He is present in his children's life, whether he is with their mother or not. He is the spiritual anchor for his children and disciplines and corrects them, but with love, dignity, and compassion. A 5:22 Man never tries to break his children's spirits because that man knows they reflect God in their life. He doesn't discourage his children; he encourages them to be the best they can be in service to their community, families, and God. A 5:22 Man teaches his son how to be a man not by his words but by his example of strength, benevolence, and compassion. A 5:22 Man teaches his daughter that she is a queen in the making, fortifying her as the beautiful queen she is and protecting her as is necessary. He is the example of the type of man that she should date and eventually marry. That is what 5:22 Men do, and it continues to the next generation of 5:22 Men and the women that love them. It starts with you, my brother. It begins with you. When you, my brother, exude Colossians 3:21, it is much easier for your children to demonstrate Colossians 3:20.

---

40 Colossians 3:21 (AMP)

Compassion for the People That Work for You

Finally, let's look at Colossians 4:1: "Masters, [on your part] deal with your slaves justly and fairly, knowing that you also have a Master in heaven."[41]

Back in the Bible days, if you worked for a king or someone with a lot of land, you were called a *slave*. If you convert this to modern times, you call that an *employee*. A 5:22 Man who has his own company or has a supervisory position at a company that is not his own should be the best employer because he knows God. He should treat his employees with compassion, dignity, and fairness. This does not mean that you sacrifice quality or let employees with bad work ethics get a pass. A 5:22 Man always operates in the spirit of excellence, and he should expect his team to do the same. However, grace and fairness should be given to those who are subordinate to you. Why? Because the 5:22 Man knows that his ultimate CEO is Jehovah Jireh. And if God treats you with fairness, dignity, and compassion, then you should extend that grace to those who work for you and with you. Once the 5:22 Man operates in Colossians 4:1, then Colossians 3:22-25 becomes easier for his employees.

It is vital for the 5:22 Man to operate in kindness in all his dealings, which can be clearly defined as benevolence and compassion. This must begin with kindness toward himself, knowing that God has been benevolent and compassionate toward him. Then those traits must extend to the man's wife, children, employees, or subordinates. Then those traits can extend to others, and you will be the true example of the 5:22 Man.

Amen!

---

41 Colossians 4:1 (AMP)

CHAPTER 6

Goodness

———◈———

Depending on how you looked at it, I was an only child and had siblings. My mother and father only had me, but when my father and mother broke up at an early age, my father met another woman who became my stepmother, and they had my younger brother, Kyle. When our father passed away, Kyle's mother, my stepmother, remarried, and her husband had two adult children, Michael and Anton, who became our stepbrothers. So depending on how you view it, I can be an only child or the middle child. I have two older stepbrothers (who I publicly say are my older brothers) and my younger brother.

Both my father and my stepfather are from the beautiful island of Jamaica. That means the Caribbean heritage and values are within me and make me who I am today. In certain parts of my life, both said, "Nothing is more important than your name." My father even told me, "Gregory, you carry my last name! When you have the name *Bloomfield*, you must walk with your head up and with pride. You don't know who I know out there on the street. So don't dutty up mi name (in his strong Jamaican accent)." If anybody reading this is from the islands, especially if you are Jamaican, then you know exactly how important your name is. I have even told both of my children the same thing. I told my son, Thaddeus, who is turning sixteen in the year that I wrote this book, and my daughter, Isabelle, who is turning fourteen in the same year, that our last name should be something to you because it is everything to me. I also told my children that I, as your father, work very hard for myself and the two of you. The reason is that I am not grinding and hustling for my first name but for *our* last name and *our* legacy. To the 5:22 Man, your legacy and your name must be of utmost importance. What you do now can set up future generations for success or failure. Your reputation is paramount, which is why goodness is essential in your 5:22 Man training

What Goodness Really Means

Please don't get sick of me with all these dictionary definitions and synonyms, but I love giving precise definitions to things to provide the proper context and perspective as we go through our 5:22 Man training. Words matter, and their meanings are important, so we understand the mission and goals we are trying to build here in the 5:22 Man journey.

Goodness is not about being a goody-two-shoes or being perfect. Not one of us men is perfect. No, not one. We are all works in progress. Some of us are in different stages in our development as men, but we all are on a journey of self-improvement (or at least we should be). If you are not, then this book is useless to you. Goodness is not about having all the answers or knowing everything there is to know. No way! When discussing goodness, we discuss four synonyms in the *Merriam-Webster Dictionary*: integrity, honesty, virtue, and morality.[42] Let us unpack these attributes one at a time and see how they apply to us, a work in progress on the journey to becoming a 5:22 Man.

---

42 Merriam-Webster Dictionary, "Goodness," https://www.merriam-webster.com/thesaurus/goodness.

Integrity

A 5:22 Man is a man that has integrity, which can be defined as "firm adherence to a code of especially moral values."[43] The key words to me are "a firm adherence to a code." The 5:22 Man believes that there are specific underlying rules that you play by. A lot of people call them "bro codes."

After my separation in 2019 and eventual divorce, I decided to work on my integrity. I decided to continue going to therapy, but this transformed into life-coaching sessions. In these sessions, I worked on my integrity by understanding what accountability and what a mature man looks like, acts like, and should react in different situations and areas such as with my finances, with my children, with my spirituality, when dealing with other men, with dating again, and so many other areas of my life. It was the best decision I made, and to this day, I have a group of male friends that hold me accountable and remind me of the importance of integrity. "A wise man will hear and increase learning, and a man of understanding will attain wise counsel."[44]

Here are some of the standard integrity codes for men that I believe the 5:22 Man should also adhere to:[45]

1. A man of integrity has unbreakable self-honesty and holds himself accountable for his actions, words, and decisions.

---

43 Merriam-Webster Dictionary, "Integrity," https://www.merriam-webster.com/dictionary/integrity.
44 Proverbs 1:5 (NKJV)
45 Paul Brian, "10 Characteristics of Men with Unwavering Integrity," Hack Spirit, last updated March 8, 2023, hackspirit.com/characteristics-of-men-with-integrity.

2. A man of integrity never fakes it. He doesn't do "fake nice." He looks people in the eyes and tells them like he sees it. Of course, he is polite, but he's not a go-along-to-get-along type of man.

3. A man of integrity apologizes when he is wrong and makes amends when he wrongs somebody. That includes his spouse, children, job, and responsibilities. He never shifts the blame, but takes responsibility and owns it.

4. A man of integrity knows how to lead wisely and by example. That means he is a leader in school, his place of employment, and especially in his marriage and within his family. He takes leadership very seriously and is a great steward of the people he vows to protect, preside over, and provide for.

5. A man of integrity behaves judiciously. In other words, he is not only an excellent leader, but he is also an excellent follower when who he is following is competent. He never follows blindly but does not behave like a rebel without a cause.

6. A man of integrity treats others respectfully but is very particular about who he opens up to. For the single man who is 5:22 in training that is looking for a relationship with a woman, he pursues her only if he is serious. He does not play games with a woman's heart, especially if she is a woman in Zion.

7. A man of integrity is faithful in romance and when he is in a relationship. Men of integrity do not commit adultery or cheat during their courtship. They do not watch

pornography or flirt with other women when they should be committed to one.

8. A man of integrity is not slothful in business. He is hardworking but knows how to balance his life between work, home, and relaxation. He looks at mistakes as learning opportunities and not as setbacks.

9. A man of integrity is consistent with his character and core values. He may appear as an entrepreneur, father, husband, friend, colleague, or many other roles, but his core values and character always remain the same and become situational.

10. A man of integrity cares about how he shows up in the world every day. He shows up to the task when others are falling asleep. He can go to bed with a clear conscience because he knows that he did not deceive people and lived his life during that day with integrity.

These are the characteristics of a man with integrity, which is a part of the goodness trait shown in the 5:22 Man.

Honesty

Tell the truth, even if the truth is not popular. We live in a culture that enjoys being lied to. We love gossip, banter, and negative things, even if we know the information could be untrue. In fact, why tell the truth when lies can be more entertaining? The 5:22 Man lives in truth. In fact, Jesus even said, "And you shall know the truth, and the truth shall set you free."[46] Because Jesus lived in truth

---

46 John 8:32 (NKJV)

and "He is the Way, the Truth, and the Life,"[47] then the 5:22 Man should strive to be honest in dealing with everyone. Remember, truth must also be coupled with compassion. A man should operate with emotional intelligence and understand how to speak the truth with love and compassion and not with brutality. However, a 5:22 Man will also do his best not to say what the other person wants to hear for fear of offending the receiver of the news.

A 5:22 Man is honest, with compassion and dignity, for the other person hearing the man's words.

Virtue

When we hear the word *virtue*, we refer to it as women, not men. After all, Proverbs 31 in the Bible is about the virtuous woman. Well, virtue does not have a gender. It is equally essential for a man to have virtue as it is for a woman. For the 5:22 Man in training, having virtue starts with what you put in your mind.

Philippians 4:8 says the following, "Finally, brethren, whatever things are true, whatever things are noble, whatever things are just, whatever things are pure, whatever things are lovely, whatever things are of good report, if there is any *virtue*, and if there is anything praiseworthy—meditate on those things."[48] Other versions of the Bible, such as the English Standard Version, say, ". . . think on those things."[49] The point is that a 5:22 Man is always conscience of what he puts in his mind. Whether it is the eye gate or the ear gate, the 5:22 Man keeps his virtue by first committing to keeping junk out of his mind. What are you listening to? Is the music you

---

47 John 14:6 (NKJV)
48 Philippians 4:8 (NKJV)
49 Ibid (ESV).

listen to helping you with your purpose and God-given destiny? Or is it causing you to be angry, lustful, or even driven to become lackadaisical in your tasks and responsibilities? Does what you listen to help you become a better husband, father, leader, and overall 5:22 Man?

Another question is, who are you listening to? I mentioned that another part of goodness is to have integrity. One essential part of integrity is having self-accountability. A way to help you with virtue is to have accountability partners. I like to call them your band of brothers that help you, coach you, pray for you, encourage you, and propel you to your next level and your God-given 5:22 Man purpose. If your circle of friends, which could include family, speak death, negativity, discouragement, jealousy, and failure over your life, then you need to change your circle of friends and pray for God to reveal true male friends that want you to succeed just as much as you want to succeed in this life and the life to come.

Finally, what are you watching on television? Are you wasting time on reality television? Are you watching shows that merely perpetuate the stereotype of African Americans that we can have money but we have no class? Are you watching programs that show death and destruction, and nothing positive comes out of it other than you feel good for a few moments? When I was looking to purchase a home, I watched more HGTV than ever. When I wanted to take my bookkeeping and tax business to the next level, I watched seminars on YouTube and attended Zoom meetings to learn more about the business and the existing opportunities. Because I wanted to be professionally creditable, I focused on returning my CPA license, which I had only renewed over thirteen years prior. That means that I had to study. I did not have time for ratchet television shows. I had to focus on my goal, which meant I had to have a Philippians 4:8 mentality. I had to monitor my thought life and guard the avenues to my heart. 5:22 Men are focused on the input into their thought life so that the outputs from that man are fruitful and beneficial to himself, his family, his career, and society.

I enjoy working out, and I began a weight loss journey recently. My weakness is sweet stuff. Juice, cookies, cakes, you name it, anything sweet is a weakness to me. I went to a nutritionist to help me with my health journey. During my consultation over the phone, she said for me to switch up the soda with sparkling water because there is less sugar. She told me to drink less juice and drink more water, and if I wanted something sweet, get some low-calorie Crystal Light or other powdered flavor and add a teaspoon of apple cider vinegar. This way, I could have the sweet with the slight taste of vinegar, which helps burn fat. She also told me to go to my kitchen cabinet, where all the cereal boxes are, and read the labels. She told me that instead of eating Honey Nut Cheerios, eat the plain Cheerios and add some fresh fruit to my cereal. My nutritionist also said not to add sugar to any cereal because there already sugar in every box of cereal you buy.

Here is my point: I had a goal, and that was to lose weight and be healthier. For me to reach my goal, I couldn't do what I used to do; I had to make some permanent lifestyle changes. When you are on a plan to be a 5:22 Man, you can't do what you used to do. You must make some permanent lifestyle changes to your social diet, your spiritual diet, your mental diet, and other areas. I had to replace sugary foods with healthier foods with less sugar. Why? Because this would help me with my goal. What people in your life do you need to replace? Please take inventory of who is in your circle and who you allow to speak in your life. Do they help you or hinder you from achieving your God-given goal as a man, to be a 5:22 Man? Are they jealous of you when you succeed, or do they celebrate with you when you reach your goal? Just like reading the label on a cereal box, we must read the labels on our friend circle, on what we read, on what we watch on television, on what podcasts we listen to, on what we watch on YouTube, on where we spend our time, on who we date, on where we go, on where we worship, on what job we take, on what school we attend, on who we let into our home . . .

You get the point. Philippians 4:8 is the guideline for virtuous living. It is not just for women; virtue is also critical for men, and it starts with what you think and meditate on.

Morality

A 5:22 Man is a man who has morals. We talked earlier about having a code in the context of integrity. However, it is also important that the code that the 5:22 Man follows supports correct behavior and does not enable wrong behavior. A 5:22 Man has a moral code based on something bigger than himself. It is based upon the Word of God. That is where his morality comes from and not from the culture or the world's standards.

Proverbs 16:25 says, "There is a way which seems right to a man and appears straight before him, but its end is the way of death."[50] A true 5:22 Man follows the Ten Commandments as his guide (if you are a Christian) and does his best to use the Word of God as his moral compass. He treats his wife correctly. He is a loving father and is present for his children. He has a good reputation in his house of

---

50 Proverbs 16:25 (AMP)

worship, marketplace, and community. In fact, the apostle Paul gave Titus some guidelines on the type of men that should be leaders in the early church. If you read the book of Titus 1:5-9, it gives us these qualifications from Paul. In summary, Paul is saying that a man in leadership should do the following:[51]

- Have unquestionable integrity
- Be the husband of one wife
- Have children who are believers and not rebellious or immoral
- Be blameless
- Not be self-willed
- Not be quick-tempered
- Have no addictions to alcohol (or other drugs and vices)
- Not be a violent person
- Be financially ethical
- Be hospitable to believers and strangers
- Be above reproach in public and in private
- Be able to teach the Word of God without errors or contradictory doctrine

This is a very long list, which means that the standard for leadership in the church (or anywhere) is very high. In the '70s, James Brown had a song called, "Pay the Cost to Be the Boss." Jesus said it another way, "To whom much is given, from him much is required."[52]

---

51 Based upon Titus 1:5-9 (AMP)
52 Luke 12:48 (NKJV)

The 5:22 Man always strives for moral excellence, and he knows that he cannot do it on his own. He needs a Divine power to assist him, and as a Christian, you can find that power from Jesus through the Holy Spirit to do the 5:22 Man work in you. Make Jesus the CEO of your personal brand, and He will lead you in true goodness, which can only come through a relationship with Him.

Amen!

CHAPTER 7

Faithfulness

As many of you know, I live in a city south of Boston called Attleboro. For many years I have had many accounting-related jobs throughout Massachusetts, primarily in the greater Boston area. I have had the opportunity to travel by car and plane to many clients in different cities throughout the United States. Some cities were Providence; Chicago; Washington, DC; and New York City. When I traveled from Attleboro to Boston, I would take the train. In Massachusetts, we called these trains *commuter rail trains*. I would run to the train stop, get on the train, show the conductor my monthly pass or individual ticket, and then sit down (and sometimes sleep). Regardless of whether I was going to work or if I was coming home from a long day, the routine was the same. Do you know what was also the same? I never saw the person operating the train and making the stops on the train line. I never questioned his pedigree to drove the train or his abilities or skill. I just ran to the train, paid my fare, and sat down until it was time to get off the train because we had reached my stop. And, yes, sometimes, I slept comfortably on that train because I had the reclining confidence that this person would get me home safely.

Some of you have a similar testimony on a train in your respective city. Allow me to give you another personal example. For the second half of 2022, I was living in two cities. I was in Massachusetts in my town of Attleboro and lived part-time in Chicago. I had a client out there where I was placed to help with their accounting operations. I was lived out there for one to two weeks at a time, and then I would come back to Massachusetts for one week to be with my children, and then I would go to Chicago again. I really like Chicago. My older stepbrother, Michael, lives out there, and a very close friend of mine is there as well (you know who you are). Whenever I needed to go to Chicago, I would drive to T F Green Airport in Providence, Rhode Island. I would park my car at the long-term parking area, take a shuttle to the airport, check in at the front desk, go through security, walk to my gate, wait for my flight, board the plane, sit in my seat, and get ready for the two-hour flight from Providence to Chicago. During the time I boarded the plane and the plane was in the air, I did not even think about whether the pilot was qualified. I never saw him fly the plane. In fact, I did not see what the pilot looked like until the plane landed and he told me, "Have a good day."

Isn't it amazing that we have faith in man to get us from one destination to another, but we struggle with having faith in God to get us through a problem in our lives? Isn't it interesting that we can easily find reclining confidence in man's inventions and abilities, but we can't trust God in His perfections and His perfect will for us? Why do we constantly struggle with trusting God but can effortlessly trust other human beings, including strangers? A 5:22 Man is a faithful man. We often think of faithfulness in your marriage, family, job, money, etc., but as important as all those elements are, we must also understand that as a 5:22 Man, your first act of faithfulness should be toward God. Once that is in place, you can easily be faithful to others. Let's talk about it.

Belief versus Faith

Many of you gentlemen reading should know by now that I am a Christian man. I have seen God move in my life, and He is still moving. I know that God is real because He has proven himself to me repeatedly. Hallelujah to His name! I also understand that not everyone is at the same level and that only some reading this book are Christians. I get it, and I appreciate you even making it this far in the 5:22 journey with me. Despite where you are in the realm of Christianity or any religion you practice, we must understand that there is a clear distinction between having belief in something and having faith in something.

Let us start with the ground floor, which is belief. *Merriam-Webster* defines belief as "a state or habit of mind in which trust or confidence is placed in some person or in something."[53] Some people do not believe in God and believe he does not exist. Most would refer to these people as *atheists*. Some people are unsure if there is a God. We would refer to them as *agnostics*. Even if you fall into those two camps, most atheists and agonists believe in something bigger than themselves. Everyone must believe in something or someone bigger than them because I believe humans were created that way. Some believe in nature, or the stars, or a family member, or their horoscopes, or a magic frog, or unicorns, or UFOs. If human beings did not believe in anything other than themselves, then why are there currently so many conspiracy theories spread around on the Internet about vaccines, the death of JFK, that Donald Trump really did win the 2020 election, and that Tupac Shakur is still alive somewhere, to name a few. People

---

53 Merriam-Webster Dictionary, "Belief," https://www.merriam-webster.com/dictionary/belief.

believe in things that they really cannot prove. So it is no shock that most people in North America, and dare I say the world, believe in God. But if you are a 5:22 Man, you realize that you can't just believe in God but must have faith in God. If you are a man who simply believes in God, then you are just a part of the culture and have the same belief system as a demon. What? Really? Yes, you have the same thinking as a demon. James 2:19 says, "You believe that there is one God. You do well. Even the demons believe . . . and tremble."[54] To become a true 5:22 Man, we must convert this belief into faith.

Faith is the belief that has been advanced from the ground floor to the penthouse. It can be defined in the dictionary as "something that is believed with a *strong conviction*."[55] Faith is "having allegiance to duty or to a person."[56] Faith is "complete loyalty to God."[57] Let me give you the Bloomfield definition of faith from my Christian experience. I believe that faith is "complete and unwavering trust and confidence in God!" You can't shake it. It is not based on what I see but on what God has told me in His word. The 5:22 Man knows that God cannot and will not lie to him. He knows that the check that God writes to him will never bounce. The 5:22 Man knows that God will never ghost him when times get bad or if he is not at his best. The 5:22 Man is assured that when things are good in his life or when things are terrible, God is with him even to the end of the age.[58] God wants us, as 5:22 Men in training, to

---

54 James 2:19 (NKJV)
55 Merriam-Webster Dictionary, "Faith," https://www.merriam-webster.com/dictionary/faith.
56 Ibid.
57 Ibid.
58 Based upon Matthew 28:20 (KJV)

transition from just believing in God to having faith in God. Why? Because it is only through faith that we can please the Lord.

"Now faith is the substance of things hoped for, the evidence of things not seen. But without faith, it is impossible to please Him, for he who comes to God must believe that He is and that He is a rewarder of those who diligently seek Him."[59]

So, my brother, let us transition from just believing in God to truly having the unwavering confidence that God will do what He said. When you change your paradigm, then you experience true faith, and then you can add faithfulness to your 5:22 experience.

Faith Is a Lifestyle

Now that we have defined what faith is, let us make this practical and actionable in our 5:22 Man journey. First, our faith in God is not a one-time event; it needs to be incorporated into our daily life. The 5:22 Man has faith as an integral part of his lifestyle. He does not just go by what he sees or even on what he hears, but the 5:22 Man lives on what God's word says and feasts on it every day through study, prayer, and lifestyle adjustments.

Habakkuk 2:2-3 says, "Write the vision, and engrave it plainly on [clay] tablets so that the one who reads it will run. For the vision is yet for the appointed [future] time, it hurries toward the goal [of fulfillment]; it will not fail. Even though it delays, wait [patiently] for it, because it will certainly come; it will not delay."[60]

The Word of God instructs the 5:22 Man to write down the visions. In other words, we as men have goals and plans for ourselves and

---

59 Hebrews 11:1,6 (NKJV)
60 Habakkuk 2:2-3 (AMP)

our future. What are your goals for the next five years if you are a single young man in college? If you know what those are, and if faith is your lifestyle, then you will have clear steps to achieve those goals. Because in verse 4, it says that "the just shall live by faith"[61]—not teach the faith, preach the faith, or talk about the theories of faith, but live by faith every day. The 5:22 Man lives by faith.

To the businessman or the entrepreneur, what is your five-year plan? Where is God telling you to go with your business? Do you have the budget and forecasts in place for your next move? Do you need to get wise counsel from experts to help you bring those visions to life? Well, write it down and take it to God in prayer for His direction and wisdom in your next move. God can speak resources to your house and send the right contractor and experts to help your business become a blessing in your respective marketplaces, communities, churches, and neighborhoods. It starts with the 5:22 Man writing down the vision, having faith that it will come to pass, and doing the work to get it to fruition.

To the 5:22 husband and the 5:22 father, as the spiritual leader of your home, what are your visions and goals for your marriage and your children? Have you written them down yet? As a leader, you must have a plan and a direction for your family. Make sure you discuss with your wife what the Lord tells you. She is your life partner, not your child or subordinate. She must feel comfortable that your vision is from God for her to feel safe to submit to you. Did you pray about it together as a family? What did God say to you about the direction of your family? Are you ready to work on your vision while trusting God for it to come to pass?

---

61 Habakkuk 2:4 (NKJV)

All these examples make your faith an integral part of your lifestyle.

Faith Is an Action Word

As I alluded to in the previous section, while you are waiting on the Lord to fulfill His promises to you as a 5:22 Man, your faithfulness to God is demonstrated when you do something regarding the revelation that God has given you for your future. A 5:22 Man is a driven man with purpose, favor, and ambition. He doesn't just talk about his future; he gets involved with working toward his future and declares that his future is right here and right now under the guidance of the Holy Spirit. He may take small, actionable steps to get closer to his God-given destiny, but he is still moving forward, even if the move is small.

The 5:22 Man's faithfulness is activated and is revving on all cylinders. In fact, you can see his faith by the way he moves. James 2:18, 20 says, "But someone will say, 'You have faith, and I have works, and I will show you my faith *by my works.* But do you want to know, O foolish man, that **faith without works is dead**?"[62] So get busy! Your works show your faith; while you are working, you have faith in God that what He said will come to pass. Your labor is never in vain when God tells you what your future will be, and when you get faith and works hooked up together, Glory to God!

Your Faith Must Be Spoken Out

In the previous chapter, I discussed who is in your circle and how important it is to watch what people say about you and your dreams. I still stand on that, and sometimes you must put up healthy boundaries against someone you know. It could be your close

---

62 James 2:18,20 (NKJV)

"friends," a sibling, or even your own parents. This is especially important when trusting God for something miraculous and huge in your life. This is when you, as a 5:22 Man, must be very careful as to who is speaking in your ear. Is this person activating your faith and starving your doubt, or is this person starving your faith and activating your doubt? Every 5:22 Man must assess and audit all his human connections when his faith is activated to believe God for the supernatural and the impossible. Without faith, it is impossible to please God,[63] and glory to His name, I want to please Jehovah every day. How about you?

The Bible records a story in Matthew chapter 8 about a centurion. You can put this book down and read the story in verses 5-13 in your own time. My favorite verses in this story are verses 8 and 10.

Verse 8: "Lord, I am not worthy that You should come under my roof. But only speak a word, and my servant will be healed."[64]

The Centurion spoke the Word in Faith, and then Jesus moved on his behalf because the Centurion's faith pleased and activated the Son of God to move on His behalf. Look at Jesus's response in verse 10: "Assuredly, I say to you, I have not found such great faith, not even in Israel."

Then in verse 13, the scripture records that Jesus healed the Centurion's servant.

Again, look at how the Centurion's faith moves Jesus to act on his request. Now, only imagine what would happen if you spoke words of faith to your situation. As a 5:22 Man, imagine that you say the Word of God back to God and remind Him of his promises. The

---

63 Hebrews 11:6 (NKJV)
64 Matthew 8:8 (NKJV)

5:22 Man speaks His faith back to the Lord, reminding Him of His Word. Look at the Son of God's response to those who have faith in Him. My brothers, this could not just happen through belief alone. But it is from the complete and unwavering trust and confidence in Christ Jesus.

My brothers, faithfulness in God will lead you to be blessed as a 5:22 Man, and that blessing will hit your family, loved ones, and associates when you can be faithful to them because you are faithful to your God. Let us remain faithful to Him as we walk on this 5:22 journey together.

Amen!

CHAPTER 8

Gentleness

———❈———

Being gentle is the most frowned upon attribute of a 5:22 Man, and it is the most counterculture. Men are not supposed to be gentle. Men are supposed to be rough, tough, brutish, and aggressive. In fact, here are some misnomers of manhood that are common in North American culture today:

- Real men must have overwhelming strength and aggression.

- Real men must have many things, such as cars and houses. They must have a ready stash of champagne bottles to toast it up and, as the youth say, "get lit."

- Real men have multiple women. The "side chick" sometimes gets better treatment than the wife (and don't forget the sneaky link).

- Real men have multiple children from multiple baby mothers. When the culture is encouraging women to be baby mothers and not wives, then there is a problem. There is an even bigger problem if the man has kids everywhere and does not care for them financially, emotionally, and spiritually. Real men take care of their children.

- Anatomy does not define real men. Yes, I said it, and I will leave it right there and move on.

With everything I just mentioned about the culturally accepted norms of manhood, why would there be room for gentleness? However, as 5:22 Men, we are going against what is popular and striving to emulate the traits of Jesus Christ, which can be found in the fruits of the Spirit.

Jesus Was Soft

The first thing I want to do is clear the misconceptions about Jesus Christ. Many people think that when men should be more like Jesus, they will be wimps, pushovers, and just soft beta men. Nothing could be further from the truth. Jesus Christ was the perfect personification of what a true man should be. Many of the paintings we see of Jesus do Him no justice. As we see in the movies, he was not a skinny white man with a beard who spoke with a British accent. Even though arguments have been made about his actual physical appearance, some things are facts:

1. **Jesus was not Caucasian** – Living in the geographical area where most of the Bible occurs, it is more believable that Jesus was a man of color, probably a Middle Eastern-looking man. He definitely did not speak in a British accent. It was likely Hebrew and Aramaic.

2. **Jesus was not skinny** – It is not believed that Jesus had a big physical stature. Think about it; he was a carpenter, so he had to have muscles to do his work. Also, he walked almost everywhere, so he had to be shredded and in great shape.

3. **Jesus was not a pushover** – Jesus clearly stood up for the oppressed, and the Pharisees and other religious leaders constantly challenged him at the time. In fact, I would say that the people that Jesus was the most critical with were the

Pharisees, the religious zealots who were pious, sanctimonious, and hypocritical. In fact, if you look at John 8:44, Jesus calls the Pharisees that were debating with them "children of the devil."[65]

Even though all these traits of Jesus disprove that he was a skinny, weak man, He still was a gentleman who exuded gentleness. The point here for the 5:22 Man is you can be both a strong physical man that commands a room and display gentleness, kindness, and class. Two things can be correct at once.

Jesus Is a Gentleman

When we speak about gentleness or, in this case, being a gentleman, what does that mean in our modern culture? We discussed goodness and kindness in the previous chapters, so I will try not to repeat myself. But *gentleness* is best defined as "being tender or showing sympathetic concern for others." Gentleness can also be demonstrated by not being aggressive in all situations but by being assertive when you need to be.

Let us look at Jesus again as an example. Now, we know that Jesus came to this Earth to save us from our sins and be our atoning sacrifice. Look at what He is saying in Revelation 3:20: "Behold, I stand at the door and knock. If anyone hears My voice and opens the door, I will come in to him and dine with him and he with Me."[66]

---

65 Based on John 8:44 (NKJV)
66 Revelations 3:20 (NKJV)

What is Jesus doing? He is knocking at the door. He is banging on the door. He is not kicking the door down. He is not aggressively ringing the doorbell. He is being calm and cool and knocking on the door to invite you and me to have a relationship with Him. This is a very important point, and it demonstrates his tenderness as a man, even though He is the Son of God with all power in Heaven and on Earth. This same Jesus turned over tables in the temple and called the religious leaders children of Satan.

The lesson to us as 5:22 Men in training is that we must know when to be tender to those who require it, which is most people, and be assertive and make a stand when it is called to be necessary. You cannot be the same in all situations because different situations call for different things. But isn't that being a hypocrite and being fake? Not at all. The reason is that Jesus is not changing his core values because of the situation; he is just applying his core values differently. Let me give you an example. I have a one-year-old goddaughter. If she has her sippy cup and spills juice on my floor in a tantrum, I will correct her and tell her that is wrong, but because she is a baby and probably doesn't know any better, I am more tender and understanding with her. She is one, not forty-one. Now, if my sixteen-year-old son looked at me and spilled juice on the floor in rebellion against me (which he has never done), the consequences would be completely different. My teenage son knows better than that, so the consequences would be different. The principle is the same: Do not spill juice on my floor. But the application of the punishment is different. If you don't know who Christ is, then His approach is different for people who are supposed to know better, like the Pharisees.

What Does This Mean for Me?

What gentleness means for me is that we should default on the side of being gentle and calm in most situations until it calls for us not to be. The 5:22 Man is a gentleman, and he is not a punk. The 5:22 Man will say good morning and good evening. He will pull chairs, open doors, and walk on the right side of the sidewalk for his lady, mother, and daughter. He will speak with the right tone for the right situation. He is humble because his mentor Jesus Christ is humble (look at Philippians 2:5-14); therefore, he emulates Him. The 5:22 Man is confident and secure in his manhood based on his relationship with God. The 5:22 Man is counterculture and responds like this:

- 5:22 Men do not lead with aggression but with integrity and become assertive if the situation calls for it.

- 5:22 Men are modest with their assets and are sensible and wise with their financial investments and spending. They also know their true wealth comes from Christ, not their checkbook.

- 5:22 Men love one woman, not breaking the hearts of many. Whether single, dating, engaged, or married, they live with integrity and gentleness, always protecting and edifying their lady, their one-and-only lady.

- 5:22 Men take care of their children and are responsible for not creating children with a woman they do not love and who does not already have their ring and their last name. They realize that child support is insufficient to raise a child if they are no longer with the mother. They are consistent with their parenting time and work daily to build a lasting legacy and inheritance for their children.

- 5:22 Men recognize that their anatomy alone does not define them as men and manhood is far more than their body. Manhood is based on how they move, act, and react in this present culture and how they show up in the world every day.

- Real 5:22 Men love Christ and want to be like him always.

CHAPTER 9

Self-Control

———— ⸻◎❈◎⸻ ————

The final attribute for the 5:22 Man in training is self-control. I know that you can have all eight previous traits listed in the earlier chapters, but if you don't master this one, it could annihilate you. As we have done in the past, let's define this term using the dictionary. *Self-control* can be defined as "the restraint exercised over one's impulses, emotions, and desires."[67] Allow me to repeat myself; if a man does not know how to master self-control and discipline himself in the critical areas of his life, he can never be a 5:22 Man. This is the most challenging part of the journey because it involves doing something and having the most accountability. The best advice that I can give a 5:22 Man in training is to ensure that you have your accountability partners or, as I have mentioned before, your band of brothers to help you stay focused and beat some of the demons you have not defeated yet in your life.

High-Value Man

In the culture, particularly in the "manosphere," there exists the term *high-value man*. When you look up that term on the Internet, many websites discuss how you can become a high-value man. Frankly, this term is very played out. Many of the people that claim

---

67 Merriam-Webster Dictionary, "Self-Control," https://www.merriam-webster.com/dictionary/self-control.

to be high-value men are not. Also, who determines our value when we use the term *high-value man*, the world, or God?

But for kicks and giggles, allow me to share some of the attributes common to describing who is a high-value man and who is not. Some of the traits that I saw online were as follows:[68]

- He is proactive.
- He has a purpose.
- He is radically self-responsible.
- He is courageous.
- He obeys a code of behavior and ethics.
- He helps his tribe survive and thrive.
- He maintains iron-clad boundaries.
- He communicates in a straightforward manner.
- He is effective and competent.
- He is formidable.
- He is committed to self-improvement.
- He is confident and believes in himself.

Most of the traits above are excellent and have merit, though there are some that I shake my head about—but that is a discussion for another day. These attributes are how other people can distinguish a high-value man. However, as a Christian, I want God to call me a

---

68 Joshua Sigafus, "12 Traits of a High-Value Man and How You Can Become One Too," The Adult Man, Last modified March 16, 2023, www.theadultman.com/live-and-learn/high-value-man.

high-value man. My value comes from something other than this list. My value comes from the Word of God.

Psalms 8:4-5 says, "What is man (that's me and my brothers) that You are mindful of him and the son of man that You visit him? For you made him a little bit lower than the angels. And You have crowned him with glory and honor."[69]

Since I am on God's mind and so are you, then I must be of high value to my Creator.

John 3:16 says, "For God so Loved the World that He gave His only begotten Son, that whoever believes in Him should not perish but have everlasting life."[70]

The fact that God gave up His Son to take my place for a death that I should have had means that I must be a high-value man to my Creator.

Romans 8:31, 38-39, "If God is for us, who can be against us? For I am persuaded that neither death nor life, nor angels nor principalities nor powers nor things present nor things to come, nor height nor depth, nor any other created thing, shall be able to separate us from the love of God which is in Christ Jesus our Lord."[71]

All these scriptures established that even before the term *high-value man* existed, I already was a high-value man because my value comes from the Lord. The 5:22 Man does not need validation from the world to say that he is high value. He inherently is a high-value

---

69 Psalms 8:4-5 (NKJV)
70 John 3:16 (NKJV)
71 Romans 8:31, 38-39 (NKJV)

person in Jesus, regardless of what the world says. Hallelujah! However, because you have inherited value as a child of God, as a 5:22 Man, you can never forget that and must cultivate practices, actions, and systems that keep you disciplined and mitigate the risk of falling into your impulses, emotions, and desires.

Self-Control Leads to Holistic Prosperity

I do not know a real man who does not want to thrive and prosper in every area of his life. I do not know a real man who does not want to do his best to protect, provide for, and preside over his family. Well, I have news for you; God also desires that for the 5:22 Man.

3 John 2 says, "I pray that you may prosper in all things and be in health, just as your soul prospers."[72]

Most people stop at verse 2 and begin to shout and dance all over the church. But they need to read verses 3 and 4 of the same single chapter of the book of Third John.

Verses 3 and 4 say that we need to "walk in the truth."[73] That means that John wants us to exercise good practices in the truth of His word to experience true prosperity, especially if we claim to be 5:22 Men or are at least striving to be. The only way we can genuinely have holistic prosperity is by exercising self-control in all areas that prosperity would have us enter.

What do I mean by *holistic prosperity*? I mean that you are blessed, sometimes in overflow, in every area God wants to bless us in. The 5:22 Man realizes that self-control is crucial for finances, but

---

72 3 John 2 (NKJV)
73 Based upon 3 John 3 and 4 (NKJV)

finances are not everything. Other areas that need to be touched are as follows:

- Spiritual
- Mental and emotional
- Physical
- Family and relational

What if I Fall? Now What?

Everyone who started this journey has taken a detour on the road or has even relapsed into some things they thought they had overcome. First of all, I want to encourage you to know that there is no condemnation of you.[74] Second, you can begin again if you own your mistake and ask the Lord to forgive you.[75] Third, you need to find your band of brothers that can help you overcome and give you some accountability so that it will not be as easy for you to fall again.[76] A common example that many men struggle with is pornography. If that is something you need help with, ask the Lord for forgiveness and ask a brother from your band of brothers to add passwords on your phone, cable box, computer, or other devices. That is being radically responsible and accountable.

Once again, you are not forgotten. God has not cut you off. You made a mistake, but you own it, and I know you will do better next time. A 5:22 Man does not stop because he has a setback. He keeps going because the Greater One lives inside of him.

---

74 Based on Romans 8:1 (NKJV)
75 Based on 1 John 1:9 (NKJV)
76 Based on 1 Corinthians 10:31 (NKJV)

Self-control is essential to master, but you don't have to do it alone. You are a 5:22 Man, and you have the power within you from the Holy Spirit to conquer anything. Remember, you are more than a conqueror in Christ.

Conclusion

At the beginning of this book, I told you how I looked in the mirror after my separation and wanted to change my life. I wanted to be a better man for me, God, my children, and my family. Well, I am happy to say that I am not perfected, but by the mercies of God, I am a different person than I was a few years ago. I give glory to God for that, and my future is brighter because I have a system and accountability to be the 5:22 Man I was called to be. You can be too.

I pray that this book helps you and is the beginning of your journey to be the man God has called you to be.

I am more than happy to come to your church or men's group to preach, share my testimony, do workshops, or serve your need where I can. If you are interested, please don't hesitate to contact me at sisterpamellapublishing@gmail.com.

Thank you so much, and may God Bless you.

Be the best 5:22 Man that you can be.

Amen!

Shalom!

About The Author

Gregory L Bloomfield

———— ⬡ ————

I was born in Toronto, Canada to a West Indian Family. My parents are both from the beautiful island of Jamaica. I am everything I am because of my Jamaican and Canadian upbringing. I currently reside in the south of Boston, Massachusetts.

As a professional, I am an accountant and a licensed CPA in the State of Massachusetts. However, my real passion is in ministry, as I am a preacher and speaker to youth, young adults and particularly men. My ministry has taken me across New England, New York, New Jersey, Florida, Canada and the United Kingdom.

I serve as an elder as the men's ministry director for the Attleboro Seventh Day Adventist church under the leadership of pastor Luis Peguero. I am also an amateur musician, as I play the saxophone and dabble with the flute, piano and drums.

My greatest pride and joy is being a single father of two teenagers, Thaddeus, sixteen and Isabelle, fourteen.

I was blessed to do my very first writing experience with DFG. It was amazing as I wrote a chapter in the book Parenting Teens: The Tug-A-War to Adulthood. Now, I am writing my first solo publication with The 5:22 Man. To God Be The Glory.

Most Importantly, I love Christ, and I am a living testimony of how God can restore someone's life from the guttermost to the uttermost.

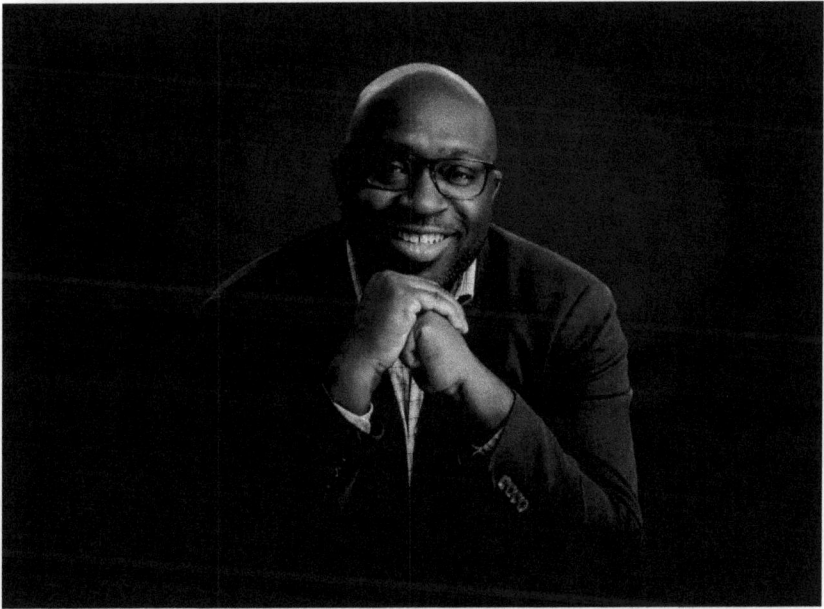

www.ingramcontent.com/pod-product-compliance
Lightning Source LLC
Chambersburg PA
CBHW072153020426
42334CB00018B/1994